DIVERGENCES

Collected Poems of
Frederic L. Johnson

Frederic L. Johnson

Order this book online at www.trafford.com
or email orders@trafford.com

Most Trafford titles are also available at major online book retailers.

© Copyright 2012 Frederic L. Johnson.

All rights reserved. No part of this publication may be reproduced, stored in a retrieval system, or transmitted, in any form or by any means, electronic, mechanical, photocopying, recording, or otherwise, without the written prior permission of the author.

Printed in the United States of America.

ISBN: 978-1-4669-7116-5 (sc)
ISBN: 978-1-4669-7115-8 (e)

Trafford rev. 12/04/2012

Trafford PUBLISHING www.trafford.com

North America & international
toll-free: 1 888 232 4444 (USA & Canada)
phone: 250 383 6864 ♦ fax: 812 355 4082

This book is dedicated to Susan and Francis Bass who helped me find the music and the rhyme.

Thank-you to my Mother, without whose support this work would never have come to be.

Contents

PART ONE: Seasons & Nature

    1. Stick Season 3
    2. Autumn 4
    3. Spring Awakens 6
    4. Spring 7
    5. The Route 9
    6. Quiet Void 10
    7. The Chilling Season 11
    8. Dog Days 12
    9. Awakening 13
  10. Dandelion 14

PART TWO: People, Places, Dreams, and Things

    1. The Cellar 17
    2. A Can of Beer 19
    3. Two Points of View 20
    4. To My Love 22
    5. The Parrot 23
    6. Universal Wonder 24
    7. Little Blessings 25
    8. The Growth of Boys 26
    9. Interim Desire 28
  10. Nightmares 30
  11. Changing Plains 31

PART THREE: Times and Tales

1. Sometime, Someplace 35
2. Assent in the Making 38
3. Night School 40
4. The Tunnel's End 42
5. A Pleasant Conversation 44
6. To A Leeward Spirit 46
7. Warning! 48
8. A Christmas Ode 49
9. Pessimism 51
10. The Wanderer 53

PART ONE

Seasons & Nature

STICK SEASON

Stately slate gray naked trees
Against a patch of dirty ashen sky
Inside dogs and cats surround me
Outside, not a squirrel, or bird to fly

The garden's gone to bed now
No white blanket yet beneath its chin
For cover in its sleeping months
Ground's too hard to see where you have been

The pellet stove puts forth its warming breeze
In the cellar bags are piled on high
The dark it now comes earlier
What was green, browns and starts to die

Snow Shovel's on the porch, scrapers in the car
Waiting for their annual vocations
Soon come hats and boots and scarves
Still put away in safe locations

Streets around here are quiet now
Summer's tourist fray has gone to ground
Just wait, but not much longer
When sleds and skis come into town

Fall's colors have abandoned us
All Hollows Eve has fled with reason
It's now the quiet graying interlude
New Hampshire calls "Stick Season"

Frederic L. Johnson

AUTUMN

The leaves are changing color
The air attracts a chill
September's now behind us
And the frosts begin to kill

Reds and gold and orange too
They won't be here for long
Will all go brown and crumble
Stampeded by the throng

It's a wild and burly season
With a harvest and a feast
Yet a time when cold is coming
And summer's warmth has ceased

Divergences

The colors bright and clear now
But what will happen in a week
It may all still be so lovely
Autumn really is a sneak

The stars they are so luminous
You can see them any night
Orion, Canis Major
Just tiny specs of light

To feel the air so crisp
And smell the change of earth
It seems to bring on sadness
And a special kind of mirth

Oh autumn is a wondrous time
So fleeting, Yet so sure
And for summer's searing heat
There is no better cure

Frederic L. Johnson

Spring Awakens

I hear the song of avian breasts
And smell the start of growth
The sun gains strength and hours
It's time that it had both

The earth is damp with warming thaw
And the trees show signs of life
Our orb begins to color some
And the winds have lost their knife

The blanket white is gone at last
Breezes tinged with renewal
And early croci show their tips
To every shirt-sleeved fool

The signs of spring abound en mass
For all the world to savor
And so we must appreciate
The good earth's greatest favor

SPRING

Green renewal I bring the earth
Colored flowers in array
Warmth and re-population
Good bye to cold and gray

I've brought the sun around again
Changed April into May
Brought out the seed and garden tools
And put the snow away

I've brought the robins back to nest
And the flora back to life
I chased away the frozen lake
And gave the sleet the knife

I've brought out all the ivies
The good ones and the bad
I am a time of happiness
And the barefoot country lad

I bring the time of "mending walls"
And also fixing roof
I really am a blazon soul
But sometimes am aloof

Frederic L. Johnson

I like to take my time with things
And never do I run
I am a time of outdoor games
And rousing romping fun

I am a rainbow bursting
To spread its wondrous hues
I am a time of fickleness
Of reds and greens and blues

But alas I'm not around too long
Before the higher heat moves in
So stop now and enjoy me
With all your kith and kin

Venture out and smell the flowers
And feel the new warm day
Before we have the dogs of summer
And I have gone away

THE ROUTE

Thinking, pondering, wondering
Climbing o'er the wall
Growing, stretching, learning
I have done them all

Laughing, crying, singing
These are daily fare
Aging, failing, dying
All to come, Beware!

Frederic L. Johnson

Quiet Void

No birds on wing, No wind
No humming planes to places far away
No voices carried from below
It is so quiet here today

No leaves as yet, No rain
No clouds to blot the blue or ray
No ring or buzz of telephone
It is so quiet here today

No grinding gears, no brakes
No slamming doors to mark the fray
No sounds of insects come to lunch
It is so quiet here today

No childish din, No sighs
No songs of love among the hay
No calls to bring on avian mates
It is so quiet here today

No thump of footsteps, No cries
No whispers that would make men gray
No nothing do I hear at all
It is so quiet here today

The Chilling Season

The sun still shines but there's no warmth
To free the earth from cold
This means that winter's on the way
So blustery and so bold

The leaves are gone and so the time
Of summer's heated charm
There's smoke in every chimney
And time on every farm

The lake is iced, the grass is brown
Awaiting snow to come
The tea is hot with honey
And sometime laced with rum

All the creatures tunneled in
To sleep the cold months through
They miss a bleak and barren time
Of blizzards and of flu

The naked branches bow and dance
To cold winds no one seen
And now the snow has come to stay
The earth just seems so clean

In winter I want summer's green
In summer icy zing
And now that fall is all but gone
Where is the smile of spring?

Frederic L. Johnson

Dog Days

When the heat is just oppressive
And the air's a wrung out sponge
The mercury's over ninety
And a pool's the place to plunge

The beach is full of bodies
And the surf is none to clean
The lake's to warm to matter
Cause the sun is downright mean

You've taken three cool showers
And you're on your fourth clean shirt
What used to be a lush green lawn?
Is now as brown as dirt

The only hope for comfort
May come with dark of night
A rumbles heard, a flash is seen
But the storm has taken flight

There's toss and turn and sweltering
Through darkness filled with wet
The light sky means its coming
Another day to sweat.

Awakening

So many little miracles
It takes to make up spring
The buds to show a tree has life
New birds to take to wing

The fragrance of the lilacs
Or the snow of apple trees
The waning of the tulips
And the warming of the seas

The profusion of the dogwood
And the greening of the lawn
The planting of the annuals
And the earliness of dawn

The sounds and smells of last night's rain
The sky both gray and blue
A breeze that doesn't chill the skin
And all just seems so new

Now man emerges from his den
At the end of winter's lair
And feels the awesome wonder
Of spring's miracles so fair

Frederic L. Johnson

DANDELION

My edges green and serrate
My center like the sun
I am that which no one wants
And I am always more than one

Some have been known to eat me
Others use me in a brew
But most just simply curse me
And all my brothers too

I'm found mostly in the suburbs
In yards both front and back
And as for great tenacity
Of that I have no lack

I like to see the spring time
And throughout the summer stay
But when its fall and I have aged
Then I just blow away

PART TWO

People, Places, Dreams, and Things

THE CELLAR

I am a place of storage
Of furnaces and dust
Of rotting unused luggage
And metals on the rust

I am a place of times gone by
Of things too small to wear
I store the fun of childhood
And the scraps of what was there

I am a place of memories
Of good times and of bad
A myriad of things tossed off
And things you wish you had

I keep the articles of time
Of past and future too
Most of them are old and used
But some of them are new

I store the seasons yet to come
And most of them gone by
The barbeque in winter
A plow when robins fly

Frederic L. Johnson

I also house the tools you use
To ease your daily grind
The washer and the dryer
And frozen food you'll find

I keep all you want tomorrow
And some things for next week
A storehouse full of wonder
For all who come and seek

Yes my walls are stone or mortar
My floor is much the same
But my heart is made in total
Of failures and of fame

So when you next come down here
To search or wash or clean
I'll show where you're going
And the places you have been

So look at this and touch of that
Remembering all the while
That I store the things that sadden
And the things that make you smile

A Can of Beer

Multicolored and cylindrical
And cold and damp to hold
Liquid gold within me
Refreshing, crisp, and bold

Frederic L. Johnson

Two Points of View

Oh when you're young and have to do
Just what your parents say
You close your eyes and wish real hard
That you'll grow up today

For at that age life seems a trap
And parents hold the key
When they say no that you can't go
You think your life not free

When you are twelve, they think you're four
And it gets worse from there
You want to date and stay out late
But nope, because the care

Now you're a teen and want to drive
A car would be so great
You ask for keys and get thin air
Again a footsore date

Divergences

And when it comes to money
For dates, must haves, and more
You have to stretch your pittance
For loans make parents sore

Oh parents rule and children serve
It's just the way things are
When we grow up we'll get our turn
Oh God, it seems so far

That's the way a child sees life
A simple sort of view
Now I'm grown and often moan
The rent seems always due

It costs to eat and have a roof
The price is very high
Now I can see just how it was
In times of days gone by

So listen, all you children
To the verses I have sung
I used to wish that I'd grow up
Now I wish that I were young

Frederic L. Johnson

To My Love

A flower in full blossom
A masterpiece unveiled
A sunset in full splendor
A mountain top unscaled

A day just full of sunshine
With a hint of mountain dew
All of these are loveliness
All of these are you

The Parrot

A voice of mumbled marbles
A fan of feathered green
A flash of yellow cresting
A marvel to be seen

Eyes of centered circles
Of white and brown and black
And in amongst the chatter
Your own words coming back

The crackling of the eaten seeds
And shells all piled up high
A view divided vertically
And never room to fly

Ever emitted upbeat sounds
Until the loss of light
The a flap and a whir
All settled for the night

A gift of nature's beauty
For all of us to share
Color, voice and caring
A friend beyond compare

Frederic L. Johnson

Universal Wonder

I sit below a starry sky
With background inky black
Wondering who there lives
And who is looking back

Are that pink or green or red
Do they have eyes or ears?
Can they talk or think or dream
Or count up time in years

Can they walk or stand up tall
Have they skin or scales
Do they breathe or take in food
And have they finger nails

Is there anyone up there?
Who resembles us at all?
Perhaps they're much much smarter
Or maybe not at all

Can it be in worlds above?
That all is peace and light
Maybe all that we do wrong
Somewhere is done right

They sit above a starry sky
With background that's unknown
Wondering just as much as I
About things they aren't shown

Divergences

LITTLE BLESSINGS

Hair of gold and eyes of blue
Cheering voices that lift the day
Little smiles looking up at you
All of these say come and play

Dirty faces and skinned up knees
These are everyday seen
Other days have party dresses
And hands and faces clean

Days of questions hard to ken
Times to have and hold
And endless stories before bed
All of these with love untold

All these things a child brings life
As they give your life a shove
And nothing ever feels so warm
As their tuck in look of love

Whether they are son or niece
Or just live in walking time
Children have the impact sure
That reduces men to rhyme

Frederic L. Johnson

The Growth of Boys

Like saplings from a yielding birch
Today young boys do grow
Not at all like days of old
So many years ago

Five, no ten, make it a score
They stood so tall and true
But alas today, I have to say
This kind have grown so few

When I was young, yes just a pup
I did my parents bidding
But there's a change in this new day
Dad works while sons are sitting

I wonder when it happened
This topsy-turvy thing
Love, respect, and yes some awe
Could these have been a fling?

I don't know just when it happened
But I think it's safe to say
It could be in the rearing
Or could the genes decay

Divergences

Some days I sit and wonder
What's happened to the lads?
They seem to stay like Peter Pan
No time for help from Dads

In these days of leaps and bounds
So little time is spent
To see them grow up strong and tall
Instead of weak and bent

Alas and sigh, It's all so true
Our boys just have it all.
Too bad it's all material
A long long way to fall

When parent's eyes are opened
And they begin to know
That boys need to be hungry
Before they'll begin to grow

Yes boys need an incentive
But not money, gifts or toys
It's lack of comfort-ability
That brings up better boys

Interim Desire

Eyes hooded with seduction
Body firm and supple
Still found in youth's own care
One should be a couple

Demure yet statuesque
Exposed and yet so sure
A blend of sweet and passion
An innocent allure

The gentle cause of spending
Nights of warm desire
Longing for entanglement
To incite a loving fire

From sole to scalp a soft caress
To place is Canaan here on earth
And so to find my arms and self
Entwined about your silken girth

Divergences

To sense the warming friction
Our dermal forms create
Surpasses all of dreamland
Are wants are all but sate

Physical is only part
Of fired up ado
Mind and soul and warmth of touch
Desirous parts of you

Your sub-cranial wonderings
Trek through night and day
If I could only find the path
That winds to its way

But alas your tenure wanes
You'll soon be miles away
Your warmth will be left only
For its sure you cannot stay

Frederic L. Johnson

Nightmares

Images in the dark
Why will there always be?
Images in the dark
Why do I always see?
Images in the dark
What do the mean to me?
Images in the dark
Are they the golden key?
Images in the dark
That sets the whole world free?
Images in the dark
Deaf to my strident plea
Images in the dark
From them, it's time to flee
Images in the dark

CHANGING PLAINS

The void, the emptiness
And all that went before
Tis sure there's no return
And there won't be anymore

Silence, deafening silence
And naught to touch or hold
All air is still and scentless
The embers have grown cold

The memories of warm caress
And aromas now gone faint
Solitude and quietness
There's not much left to taint

Many nights of war encasement
Dwindled down to one's own feel
Days long gone of free abandon
Life's a dream of youth's lost zeal

Looking back, life's last pleasures
It's just a mix of yore and dreams
Today the joys are just some smaller
While yesterday they came in reams

Time has come to choose a new path
Shuck the past and climb on high
Ne'er forget the aces and passion
They're the wings on which you fly

PART THREE

Times and Tales

Sometime, Someplace

The sound is all around me
Like a heavy coat and veil
I'm feeling almost stifled
I yearn for hill and dale

The air seems thick and clinging
And full of foreign smells
What happened to the countryside?
With its daisies and blue bells

I used to know the country
Where the sky was blue not gray
But now I know the urban life
Where you breathe your life away

I wonder how it happened
This growing city thing
It must be economics
That puts us in the sling

To give up years and health and looks
To live where money grows
It seems to me a stupid thing
But life deals out rough blows

Frederic L. Johnson

Yes one must eat and have a roof
Stay warm and pay bills too
We all must have our job in life
So each can pay their dues

There is no other reason
We do because we must
Plug on and keep a going
Till our return to dust

But though we do not what we like
We all can dream and so
We have a way of rising up
When life has dealt us low

For me it's simple country life
A quiet living place
Where days are days and months are months
An easy kind of pace

Divergences

Someday I know I'll get there
Leaving all that stinks behind
I'll breathe clean air and eat fresh food
And sleep with peace of mind

Oh yes I love the country
It's a place where air is fresh
But now I'm stuck to make a buck
In a jungle made of flesh

But I'll not be here forever
As long as I can dream
And when my work is over
I'll get out this torrent stream

I'll go out in the country
And run throughout the hay
I'll sit me by a quiet stream
And there forever stay

Frederic L. Johnson

Assent in the Making

When once a deed is measured
And the good of it is done
The war is not yet over
And the battle's just begun

Oh men must die and women mourn
For those no longer here
And yet it seems so far away
That day, that month, that year

The fight's a long and hard one
It seems to ever be up hill
At times you feel you can't go on
And yet you know you will

For our time is not yet over
And our work is not yet done
We've got along long way to go
Before the setting sun

We're half way up the mountain
It's a steep and fearful trail
And all the world seems watching
Lined up on hill and dale

Divergences •

We've almost made the top now
Our feet begin to slip
We might have fell the whole way down
If not for one small lip

We caught a ledge and held on tight
No further did we fall
For the bottom's not the place for us
We've got to stand up tall

There were two choices we could see
To stay or start a new
So we climbed a rock and carried on
The clouds came into view

Today we still are climbing
And soon we'll make the top
We'll climb and fall, and climb and fall
And never never stop

For failure's just not in us
We've got to plug on through
Someday we'll find our place in life
Our faith will ere be true

Frederic L. Johnson

NIGHT SCHOOL

When once you're hooked on learning
And intent on inner growth
You'd like to give up working
But you know you must do both

For schooling is of two tiers
Of learning and finance
The former is a pleasure
The latter is the lance

To pay for nightly pleasure
You work throughout the day
And all the time you wonder
Is there not a better way

To get up every morning
Becomes the day's first chore
This is just the first step
That leads to many more

For the day has too few hours
Are there really twenty-four
By the time you've reached the school
You could sleep right on the floor

And now comes the professor
Who expects that you will know?
All that she discusses
For your grade cannot be low

She would like to see some bright eyes
And maybe full blown sails
Alas most often what she gets
Is simply dragging tails

You try to keep your head up
And take in all you can
Using all your will to make it
There goes the best laid plan

When finally the clock strikes
And it's time that you can rest
You've got to do your homework
Another hard fought quest

So now in the wee hours
You on the pillow lay your head
Too soon will come the morning
And you will have to leave your bed

Oh yes, an education
Is a worthy thing to seek?
Even if you always feel
That you could sleep a week

Frederic L. Johnson

The Tunnel's End

When the day is gray and dragging
And the sun just won't come out
You wonder where you're going
And what life's all about

When you day is just not working
And the car has got a flat
You think that objects hate you
And your shoulder's to the mat

When you've read someone the riot act
And you're stuck will all you've said
You wish it all would go away
And you should have stayed in bed

When you know the car needs tuning
And the laundry's piled up high
Your homework isn't finished
And the deadline's going by

Divergences

When you'd like to be relaxing
But you know you have to work
And you'd like to see a smile
But all you gets a smirk

When your body's just not with it
And your feet begin to ache
You want to have some solitude
But there's still a life to make

Now just when you are worn and weary
And somewhere near your end
You hear a sound unlike the rest
And you begin to mend

It is a sound of warmth and light
So wondrous and so pure
It is a sound like laughter
An omnipotent cure

What is this sound so lifting?
That it can upward send
It is the voice one only knows
When one hears from a friend

Frederic L. Johnson

A Pleasant Conversation

Once two though just acquainted
Sat down to dine and chat
The ale rained down in pitchers
And words flew off the bat

It was a planned discussion
Taking weeks to bring about
Add ale to tongues so crafter
Of depth there was no doubt

The evening started early
But carried very late
Setting was an Irish Pub
The goal was just to sate

I knew so little of him
And he knew naught of me
We both began of background
Frist I and then came he

We talked throughout the evening
And on into the night
Stopping only for some nourishment
And urinary flight

Divergences

We emptied numerous pitchers
And dined on Fruits de mer
Our host began to dim the lights
So we left him what was fair

The discussion changed its venue
To the habitat he leased
And just for love a moment
The conversation ceased

It soon was back and full of song
Of works both old and new
The hour crept toward the dawn
Biko-Biko filled the view

Then came the time for parting
For the clock was striking two
What started as an acquaintance?
Ebbed into friendship true

I gave him a small token
A gesture which felt right
Hands were shook in value
And I left into the night

When next I was awaking
And the sunlight filled the skies
I had little memory of our chat
To nobody's surprise

Frederic L. Johnson

To A Leeward Spirit

The music of another time
Drifts down the hall so free
But the soul from whom the music comes
Has half the years of me

How can she know the era?
In which these songs saw life
A time of disagreement
And days so full of strife

Can she know to what degree?
This music led the way
Through sit-ins and the riots
Mainstays of the day

Around the time that she was born
We closed a school to show
The government had gone astray
And also "We won't go!"

Divergences

It's more than just the music
She's just plain out of time
Most of what she sees as hers
Was years ago all mine

It's nice to be reminded
Of youthful years gone by
And know they're not forgotten
As the music just won't die

So I thank my newest neighbor
For the gift of slowing time
And in return I do submit
My thanks in form of rhyme

Frederic L. Johnson

WARNING!

When anger reaches boiling point
And fisticuffs are near
It's time to give a man some space
Or touch the heat and sear

When ears are deaf and eyes too fail
Know trouble's on the way
You better keep some distance
Till reason comes to play

When tongues begin to work too hard
And thought and senses pale
You had better find a place to hide
That only you can scale

For temper can come in short ones
It can stay for just a sec.
But just what comes when it erupts
Can make you hit the deck

So if you feel the heat arising
And control has gone astray
Don't try to talk or reason
Just simply walk away

A Christmas Ode

When all around is a piney smell
And the world seems white and green
The night is made of colored lights
To make a Christmas Scene

It is a time of ringing bells
And busy shopping malls
A time to gather family
And hang up shiny balls

One sees the smiling faces
Of those on Santa's knee
And a star up in the heavens
That was placed for you and me

It is a time of reaching out
With cards and gifts and more
When the air is full of carols
And the lock is off the door

Frederic L. Johnson

A time for anticipation
And thoughts of folks gone by
A time of love and charity
A night when reindeer fly

You can hear the children stirring
Though it's only five o'clock
The snow outside is falling hard
You can barely see a block

There are presents to be opened
And a turkey for the meal
Wonders to be savored
And surely, it's all real

Yes, it is the Christmas season
With lots to see and hear
So have a Merry Christmas
And a wonderful New Year!

Divergences

Pessimism

The summer goes a whizzing by
Clouds and robins fill the air
On the earth we do rely
And here, alone, stand I

On the brink of a new day
Miles to go, on my way
It's all a blur I say
But I want it all that way

And now's the edge of inky night
There's a limit to my sight
Hard to tell wrong from right
I keep chasing after might

Working, sleeping, handling fear
Why's there always no one here
Like it when there's someone near
To put my arms round someone dear

Frederic L. Johnson

All goes on as I began
Yes confusion makes the man
Always take all we can
Books, Ideas, burn and ban

All around, we steal and rook
Never enough, what all we took
Samaritan gets a dirty look
Never shocked, never shook

The winter slowly eking by
Only snowflakes in the sky
Just on yourself you can rely
And still here alone, stands I

The Wanderer

When once there was a young gay man
Of melancholy mind
He roamed about this vast green earth
For peace and love to find
He came to know a simple truth
A pure and honest kind
That he'd never get just what he sought
If only he just pined
And now we find this young gay man
Forever on the road
He never settles in one place
Or rests his weary load
He always hoped to meet one man
Of true and honest code
But he must keep on searching
And not let the trail go cold
The young gay man grows tired
His step has lost its spring
Even though the sun is shining
And the sparrow's on the wing

Frederic L. Johnson

Up a head the paths diverge
And he begins to sing
For he knew which ever path he chose
The truth would simply ring
And now the young gay man grows old
Too many years gone by
His many decades on the hunt
Have all just seemed to fly
But the path he chose has done him well
With a loved one he does lie
Ending all his lonesome travels
With one contented sigh
Ending all his lonesome travels
With one contented sigh . . . .

Made in the USA
Middletown, DE
01 December 2023